THE JOURNEY
LIVING THIS NEW LIFE

CASEY TREAT

The Journey (Living This New Life)

ISBN: 978-1-927529-65-2
January 2019
MacKenzie Publishing

Originally published by Casey Treat & Christian Faith International
as:
Living the New Life, 1990
ISBN 0-931697-17-4

MacKenzie Publishing

TABLE OF CONTENTS

INTRODUCTION

Being born of the Spirit and filled with the Spirit are the greatest events of your life. These experiences change your eternal destiny as well as your daily life.

I am praying this book will start you on a journey with God that will bring great fulfillment to your life both now and forever.

Casey Treat

BECOMING BORN AGAIN

I'll never forget the first day I walked into an alive church service. Everything about it was new and strange to me. Not only did I not know many people, but I did not understand most of what they said. The Christian church has many words that are uncommon to most people. That's why I wrote this book—to assist you in understanding what the words "born again" mean and how to **Live This New Life**.

In the next few pages, you'll learn why every person must be born again, how to be born again, and what it means to be born again. You will also gain some insight on what to do now that you are born again so that you can live a happy, successful Christian life.

The Scripture verses in this book are from The New International Version Bible. Other translations that are good to study are the King James Version, the Amplified Bible, and The New American Standard Bible.

If you do not know where the different books of the Bible are, look in the front of your Bible and you will find a list of the books contained in the Bible. Go to the page listed there and you will see chapter and verse numbers. A reference such as John 3:3 means you will find that verse in the Book of John, chapter three and verse three.

Why Must Every Person Be Born Again?

Jesus was the first person to use the words "born again." He was speaking to a very high religious officer named Nicodemus and said, "Unless a man is born again, he cannot see the kingdom of God." (John 3:3).

Nicodemus thought Jesus was talking about a second physical birth so he did not understand. Many people today think as Nicodemus did and try to figure out exactly what this new birth is all about.

Jesus then went on to explain, "Flesh gives birth to flesh, but the Spirit gives birth to Spirit" (John 3:6).

This means that physically speaking we were already born, but spiritually speaking we still need to be born. Our physical body is born, but our human spirit is not. When Adam rejected the

Lord and obeyed the devil (Genesis 3), he died spiritually. God told Adam, "But you must not eat from the tree of the knowledge of good and evil, for when you eat of it you will surely die" (Genesis 2:17).

We know that Adam did not physically die on that day, for he lived to be 930 years old. What died that day was Adam's spirit man. That is, the real person that lives on the inside of the body. Your body is a house in which the real you, a spirit man, lives.

When Adam's Spirit died, he was spiritually separated from the Father God. From that point on, all his children were born spiritually dead and separated from God. Natural men have no fellowship or right standing with the Father. This is apparent by looking at all the ungodly things happening in the world today.

When Jesus told Nicodemus, "You must be born again" (John 3:7), He was saying that every man is already physically born, but he must be spiritually born in order to go to heaven. Without being born again, you have no fellowship with the Lord; therefore, you have no relationship. You can go to church, read the Bible, and be a good person, but unless the spirit is born again, you cannot go to heaven nor have fellowship with the Lord. Jesus did not suggest that people be born again. He strongly said, "You must be born again."

This commandment cannot be avoided if you want a relationship with the Lord Jesus and the Father. Those who refuse to be born again will never have eternal life and will never have a relationship with the Father God. When they die physically, they will be separated from God for eternity and exist in the torment of hell forever.

Those who are born again have eternal life. Jesus said, "I tell you the truth, whoever hears my word and believes him who sent me has eternal life and will not be condemned; he has crossed over from death to life" (John 5:24).

They will never die spiritually. When their physical body stops functioning, they will meet the Lord in heaven and live with Him throughout eternity.

How to Become Born Again

The Bible is the foundation for everything the Christian believes. What we feel or think is not always the truth, but the Word of God is. Therefore, we must look to the Word to find out how to become born again. 1 John 5:1 says, "Everyone who believes that Jesus is the Christ is born of God."

This is the basic principle of how to become born again. There are several points within this simple statement that you must understand.

1. It's for everyone.

Notice that Salvation or the New Birth is not limited to a certain group of people. It matters not what age, color, culture, or social class that you have come from; there is not one person who cannot become born again. The Apostle Peter said, "And everyone who calls on the name of the Lord will be saved" (Acts 2:21).

You are an "everyone," so you are included in those who can become born again.

2. **You must believe.**

This does not mean to just think about something. To believe in Jesus means to have faith, confidence, and trust in Him. The Bible teaches that faith has corresponding actions. "In the same way, faith by itself, if it is not accompanied by action, is dead" (James 2:17).

Some people think that as long as they say they believe in Jesus, they will go to heaven no matter how they live. They have the attitude that it is okay for a Christian to drink, smoke, lie, be lazy, and have negative behavior. They think that as long as they believe, they will go to heaven. You can see how that is wrong. When you believe in Jesus, you will act the way He did. You will live the kind of life that Jesus lived on earth.

Of course, not all of us are perfect, and there will always be things we are changing in order to grow. It is important to realize that believing also requires action.

3. **You must say it.**

When you believe in Jesus as your Lord and Savior, it will come out of your mouth. Paul said we must "confess with our mouth 'Jesus is Lord'."

In Matthew 10:32-33, Jesus said, "Whosoever therefore shall confess me before men, him will I confess also before my Father which is in heaven. But whosoever shall deny me before men, him I will also deny before my Father which is in heaven" [King James Version (KJV)].

Part of being born again is confessing before others that Jesus is our Lord and that we will follow Him.

4. Jesus is Lord.

This means that Jesus is the Messiah, Savior, or Lord. There is no other person or god that holds this position. Only Jesus is Savior; only He is Lord over all the earth. Talking about Jesus in Acts 4:12, Peter said, "Salvation is found in no one else, for there is no other name under heaven given to men by which we must be saved."

Jesus is not "a" way to heaven or "one" way to heaven; **He is the only way**. He said in John 14:6, "I am the way and the truth and the life. No one comes to the Father except through me."

When you believe in Jesus as the Christ, you make Him the Lord of your life. That means He is the supreme authority, master, or boss of your life. If Jesus is not your Lord, you are not born again.

Paul said in Romans 10:9, "That if you confess with your mouth, 'Jesus is Lord,' and believe in your heart that God raised him from the dead, you will be saved."

When you say, "Jesus is Lord," that is a confession of submission. You are turning your life over to Jesus and now He is your supreme authority. A Christian does not do his own thing and live like the world. The Bible says we are not to live our lives like other people who are not born again. When Jesus is Lord, we will follow His standards for our life and obey His teachings in the Bible. Sometimes you may not feel like doing what it says in the Word, and it may not be the easiest way, but it is the Christian way. When Jesus is Lord, He is Master and Leader of all we do.

When you believe in your heart and confess "Jesus is Lord," God does something inside you. The real you, the spirit man, is recreated and becomes alive. Remember, Jesus said, "...the Spirit gives birth to spirit" (John 3:6).

The Holy Spirit comes into your life and causes your human spirit to be born again. This is not something you can figure out with your mind—it is a spiritual fact. 2 Corinthians 5:17 tells us, "Therefore, if anyone is in Christ, he is a new creation; the old has gone, the new has come!"

When you believe in Jesus and confess Him as your Lord, you are changed inside. Not your body and not your mind, but the real you, the spirit man. You probably won't feel any differently, and you won't look any different; but, spiritually speaking, you are a new creature! You are no longer separated from God. You now are born of the Holy Spirit. You have fellowship with the Father and Jesus. Your name is written in The Book of Life, and you are a part of the family of God.

Let's pray this simple prayer to become born again. Say it out loud and with sincerity.

"God, I believe Jesus is raised from the dead and is alive right now. I confess Jesus is my Lord and Master of my life. Thank you for my salvation. Amen."

Being Baptized in Water

One of the first steps to take after you are born again is to be baptized. You may think, "Why do I have to be baptized?" or "My parents baptized me when I was a baby."

Let's take a look at what the Bible has to say about baptism.

1. **Water baptism is to take place after you are born again.**

   In Acts chapter 8, Philip, an evangelist, told an Ethiopian eunuch the good news about Jesus.

   "As they [Philip and the eunuch] traveled along the road, they came to some water and the eunuch said, 'Look, here is water. Why shouldn't I be baptized?' Philip said, 'If you believe with all your heart you may.'

The official answered, 'I believe that Jesus is the son of God'" (Acts 8:36-37).

Notice Philip said, ***"If you believe with all your heart, you may."*** We believe *first* and then are baptized.

Infants and small children are not yet able to confess Jesus as their Lord and Savior and should not be baptized. We are to pray over our infants and dedicate them to the Lord. Jesus said, "Let the little children come to me and do not hinder them, for the kingdom of God belongs to such as these. I tell you the truth, anyone who will not receive the kingdom of God like a little child will never enter it" (Mark 10:14-15).

After our children are old enough to become born again, they are able to be baptized.

It is God's will that believers are baptized in water after they are born again. "He [Jesus] said to them, 'Go into all the world and preach the good news to all creation. Whoever believes and is baptized will be saved, but whoever does not believe will be condemned'" (Mark 16:15-16).

2. **Although you are commanded to be baptized, baptism alone will not save you.**

When Jesus was being crucified, one of the criminals hanging on the cross next to Him said, "'Lord, remember me when thou comest into Your kingdom.' And Jesus said to him, 'Verily I say unto thee, today shalt thou be with Me in Paradise'" (Luke 23:42, 43 KJV).

The criminal did not have the opportunity to come down off the cross and be baptized. However, he confessed Jesus as Lord. And Jesus told him, ***"Today you will be with Me in Paradise."***

This does not mean that we are only baptized if we want to be. Jesus commanded, "Therefore go and make disciples of all the nations, baptizing them in the name of the Father and of the Son and of the Holy Spirit" (Matthew 28:19).

3. **Baptism is an outward expression of our salvation and our obedience to the Lord Jesus Christ.**

When we are baptized, we are immersed or totally submerged in water. The story in Acts tells us that when Philip baptized the eunuch, "Then both Philip and the eunuch went down into the water and Philip baptized him" (Acts 8:38).

Notice that they went *down into* the water, and in verse 39 it says *they came up out of* the water. It is important that we say stay scriptural instead of following religious traditions.

4. **Water baptism is an outward sign of what has happened inwardly after we are born again.**

"Don't you know that all of us who were baptized into Jesus Christ were baptized into his death? We were therefore buried with him through baptism into death in order that, just as Christ was raised from the dead through the glory of the Father, we too may live a new life" (Romans 6:3-5).

Our submersion is a symbol of the death of our old self, and our coming out of the water is a symbol of the new life Jesus has given us.

RECEIVING THE BAPTISM OF THE HOLY SPIRIT

This section was written to help God's people receive the fullness of life in the Spirit. Many born-again people think they have received all that God has, but they are not entering into the fullness of the Holy Spirit. It is one thing to be "born" of the Spirit, but it is another thing to be "filled" with the Spirit.

The baptism with the Holy Spirit is a necessary part of the successful Christian life. Jesus did not suggest to His disciples that they be baptized with the Holy Spirit. He commanded them to wait in Jerusalem and go nowhere until they had been endued (filled) with the power from on high. If we are disciples of Jesus, that commandment is still for us today. Jesus wants you to be filled with the

Holy Spirit and receive the power therein to live victoriously in every aspect of life.

In the pages to come, you will learn what the baptism with the Holy Spirit is, how to receive it, and how it will benefit your life according to the Word of God. Throughout this section, I will use the specific terms "baptized with the Holy Spirit," "baptized with the Holy Ghost," and "filled with the Spirit" interchangeably as the Bible does; they all mean the same thing.

What Is the Baptism with the Holy Spirit?

The baptism with the Holy Spirit is a filling of the whole life of a believer with the supernatural power of the Spirit. We are **born** of the spirit to be part of God's family. We are **filled** with the spirit to be victorious and fruitful in God's family.

In the last hours of Jesus' ministry on earth, He left explicit directions with His followers: "I am going to send you what my Father has promised; but stay in the city until you have been clothed with power from on high" (Luke 24:49).

"He [Jesus] gave them this command: 'Do not leave Jerusalem, but wait for the gift my Father promised, which you have heard me speak about. For John baptized with water, but in a few days you will be baptized with the Holy Spirit...you will receive power when the Holy Spirit comes on you; and you will be my Witnesses in Jerusalem, and in all Judea and Samaria, and to the ends of the earth'" (Acts 1:4-5, 8).

He commanded them to wait until they were filled with the Holy Ghost. If it was that important to Jesus, it should be that important to us. The 120 men and women who believed in Jesus did what He said. They stayed together in an upper room and prayed in one accord, waiting for what Jesus had told them would happen.

The Bible tells us what happened after they had waited for ten days: "When the day of Pentecost came, they were all together in one place. Suddenly a sound like a blowing of a violent wind came from heaven and filled the whole house where they were sitting. They saw what seemed to be tongues of fire that separated and came to rest on each of them. All of them were filled with the Holy Spirit and began to speak in other tongues as the spirit enabled them" (Acts 2:1-4).

The day of Pentecost was a Jewish feast day that came fifty days after the Passover feast, which is when Jesus was crucified. God chose this day to release the fullness of the Holy Spirit in the lives of those believers. Notice that they were **all** filled with the Holy Spirit; men, women, old or young, they **all** received. This was the beginning of the New Testament church age, which we are now in.

We are a part of the same church these 120 people were. We have the same Father, same Savior, same Spirit, same Word, and same face. They were the beginning of what is still happening today. The experience of the new birth and the baptism of the Holy Spirit will go on, just like Acts chapter 2, until Jesus returns.

Not the New Birth

Let's talk about what the Holy Spirit is not. To be filled or baptized with the Holy Spirit is not the same as being born of the Spirit. It is one thing to be born; it is another thing to be filled. Jesus said, "I tell you the truth, unless a man is born again, he cannot see the kingdom of God" (John 3:3).

Then He explained it further in John 3:6, "Flesh gives birth to flesh, but the Spirit gives birth to spirit."

Being born again or born of the spirit happens when individuals make Jesus their Lord and the supreme authority of their lives by confessing with their mouths and believing in their hearts according to Romans 10:9. This is what makes us Christians part of God's family. This new birth is an act of the Holy Spirit imparting life or God's nature to our human spirit. When the Holy Spirit, or the life of God, comes in contact with our dead human spirit, change takes place. We are recreated spiritually. Paul said it like this, "Therefore, if anyone is in Christ, he is a new creation; the old has gone, the new has come" (2 Corinthians 5:17).

Any man or woman in the world can be born again at any time. It is done by making Jesus your Lord and Savior. Jesus said in John 14:16-17 (KJV), "And I will pray the Father and He shall give you another Comforter, that He may abide with you forever; even the Spirit of truth; whomever the world cannot receive, because it sees Him not, neither knoweth him, but you know Him; for he dwells within you and shall be in you."

Notice while talking about the Holy Spirit in this verse He said that the world **cannot receive Him**. This "other comforter" could not be the act of being born again because we were all in the world before we were born again. To receive what Jesus is talking about here, you must first get out of the world and into God's Kingdom. He is speaking of the baptism with the Holy Spirit. When a person is born again, they are no longer a part of the world and are now able to receive the Spirit of Truth or the Holy Ghost.

This is not to say that born-again people do not have the Holy Spirit at all. They are born of the Spirit, but they don't have the full release of the Spirit in their lives. This takes place when they are baptized with the Holy Ghost.

John the Baptist told the people about the ministry of Jesus in John 1:33, "I would not have known him, except that the one who sent me to baptize with water told me, 'The man on whom you see the Spirit come down and remain is he who will baptize with Holy Spirit.'" Notice that Jesus is the baptizer with the Holy Spirit."

To be born again is something that the Holy Spirit does. To be baptized with the Holy Spirit is something that Jesus does. Jesus is the Baptizer with the Holy Ghost.

Even after reading these verses, some individuals will still have the idea that we are born again and that's all there is. Let's look at a story that took place in the early church recorded in Acts chapter 8. An evangelist, named Philip, had gone down to Samaria and preached Jesus to the people there. The Bible said he had good results (Acts 8:5-8). Many of the people were born again and baptized in water. "But when they believed Philip as he preached the good news of the kingdom of God and the name of Jesus Christ, they were baptized, both men and women" (Acts 8:12).

While this revival was still going on in Samaria, word got back to Jerusalem about what was going on. So, Peter and John came down to help out with the ministry. I want you to notice why they came. "When the apostles in Jerusalem heard that Samaria had accepted the word of God, they sent

Peter and John to them. When they arrived, they prayed for them that they might receive the Holy Spirit" (Acts 8:14-15).

Many of the people already believed in Jesus. They were born again and even baptized in water, but they didn't have all that God had for them. If they had received it all when they were born again, Peter and John would not have come down to pray for them to receive the Holy Ghost. Acts 8:16 says, "...the Holy Spirit had not yet come upon any of them; they had simply been baptized into the name of the Lord Jesus."

It is one thing to be born of the Spirit; it is completely different to be filled with the Spirit.

In traveling to Ephesus, Paul found several disciples. He had fellowship with them and right away sensed something was missing in their Christian experience, so he asked them, "Did you receive the Holy Spirit when you believed?" (Acts 19:2).

Paul knew that being born again was not all that God had for His people. He wanted these disciples to not only believe in the Lord Jesus but also to be baptized with the Holy Ghost. If they were the same experience, he would not have asked if they had received the Holy Ghost.

We have millions of Christians who believe in Jesus, but they have not received the baptism with the Holy Spirit. I pray they might hear the truth and receive the fullness of what God has for them.

The First Evidence

There is an initial evidence that takes place in the life of the believer when they are filled with the Holy Spirit. It is not a physical feeling. Some have thought (or have been told) that when you are filled with the Spirit "you will feel power go through you," "lightning bolts will go through your body," "glory balls will burst on your head," "shivers will go up your spine," or "the power of God will knock you to the floor."

You may have heard one or more of these and they are lies. **Nowhere in the Bible is a physical feeling associated with the baptism of the Holy Spirit**. You do not feel the Spirit physically. (This is not to say that you never will, but a physical feeling associated with the Holy Ghost is not a normal occurrence.)

Others have said that when you are filled with the Spirit you'll never sin again or have any problems in your life. This is also a lie. The baptism with the Spirit will not instantly transform you into an angel and remove every negative circumstance. There will be positive changes because God's power is released in you but not one big metamorphosis.

The initial evidence of being baptized with the Holy Spirit is that you will begin to speak with other tongues. Notice what Acts 2:4 says: “All of them were filled with the Holy Spirit and began to speak in other tongues as the Spirit enabled them.”

They didn't roll on the floor, bark like a dog, climb the walls, hang from the chandelier, or foam at the mouth. They began to speak something. It was the language of the Holy Spirit, which the Bible calls other tongues. They were all sitting in prayer, not rolling, not jumping, not kneeling—sitting. And, when they were filled with the Spirit, they began to speak with other tongues. This is the initial or first sign of being baptized with the Holy Spirit. Let's look at other Bible passages that state this.

One day Peter went to the house of a Gentile named Cornelius, who had been seeking God. An angel headed toward Cornelius to send for Peter, so when Peter came, he began to teach them all about Jesus. He told how Jesus was the anointed one, and how he had healed all who were oppressed of the devil.

The Bible says, "While Peter was still speaking these words, the Holy Spirit came to all who heard the message. The circumcised believers who had come with Peter were astonished that the gift of the Holy Spirit has been poured out even on the Gentiles. For they heard them speaking in tongues and praising God" (Acts 10:44-46).

Notice that the Holy Ghost fell on those who heard the Word, and all the Jews were astonished. How did they know the Holy Ghost had filled them? Did they see Him? Did they feel Him? No, verse 46 gives that answer. "For (or because) they heard them speaking in tongues and praising God." The first thing that happened to these people when they were baptized with the Holy Spirit is they began to speak with other tongues.

Again, in Acts 19, Paul ministered to some people in Ephesus. They had been baptized by John in water for repentance, but they knew nothing of the Holy Spirit. Acts 19:5-6 tells us: "On hearing this, they were baptized in the name of the Lord Jesus. When Paul placed his hands on them, the Holy Spirit came on them, and they spoke in tongues and prophesied."

This situation was no different than the others. The first thing that happened when they were filled with the Spirit was they spoke with tongues. This is the initial evidence. Jesus said, "Every matter may be established by the testimony of two or three witnesses" (Matthew 18:16).

I have given three passages (witnesses), so if you are scriptural, you must believe that speaking with tongues is for all who are filled with the Holy Spirit.

Some have said, "Tongues are of the devil!" That's a statement of Bible ignorance. People are afraid of what they don't understand, so they do anything, including lie, to avoid it. Paul said, "I thank God that I speak in tongues more than all of you" (1 Corinthians 14:18).

It's obvious Paul didn't believe tongues were of the devil. Some say, "I'll never go around any tongue talkers." Well, they will have a hard time in heaven being around Paul, Barnabas, Peter, John, Philip, Matthew, and Mary (Jesus' mother); *they all spoke with other tongues.*

Who Is the Baptism of the Holy Spirit For?

There are those who believe in being filled with the Spirit, but they say it is not for everyone. Let's check the Bible and see what God says. I am always more interested in what God's Word says than in what anybody else says.

John the Baptist said, "The next day John saw Jesus coming toward him and said, 'Look, the Lamb of God, who takes away the sin of the world!' I would not have known him except that the one who sent me to baptize with water told me, 'the man on whom you see the Spirit come down and remain is he who will baptize with the Holy Spirit'" (John 1:29, 33).

He said Jesus would take away the sin of the world and baptize believers with the Holy Ghost. Whom is He going to baptize with the Holy Ghost? The same people He took the sin away from. He provided the baptism with the Holy Spirit for them, too. Whoever will accept the forgiveness of sin that Jesus provided can also have the baptism with the Holy Ghost that Jesus provides.

In Acts 2:38-39, the Bible says, "Peter applied, 'Repent and be baptized, every one of you, in the name of Jesus Christ so that your sins may be forgiven. And you will receive the gift of the Holy Spirit. The promises for you and your children and for all who are far off—for all who the Lord of our God will call.'"

He said whoever would repent (be born again) and be baptized in water would receive the gift of the Holy Ghost. Then, to make it clear that this was for everyone, He broke it down in detail.

Promises for:

1. You (all who were present);

2. For your children (all those born or not yet born);

3. All who are far off (everyone on earth at that time); and

4. For all whom the Lord Our God will call (all who would be born again throughout time).

No one is left out. The baptism with the Spirit is for all people.

Jesus said in Mark 16:17, "And these signs will accompany those who believe: In my name they will drive out demons; they will speak in new tongues."

Whoever **believes** will speak with new tongues. The only people who do not speak with tongues are those who do not believe. God can't make you do anything. You receive His gifts by faith. If you don't believe, you don't receive.

Someone said, “If God wants me to speak with tongues, He'll make me.” Wrong! Jesus said, *“This sign will follow those who believe.”* In His name they will speak with new tongues.

And in 1 Corinthians 12:30, when Paul asks, “Do all speak in tongues?”, he is speaking of the gifts of diverse kinds of tongues that are to be interpreted in the church service. This is one of the nine gifts of the Spirit listed in the chapter for the body of Christ. He is not speaking of the personal gift of tongues for the believer. They are **two different things**. It is just like the gift of faith listed in 1 Corinthians 12. All believers do not have diverse kinds of tongues that will be spoken out and interpreted by the body, but all can have the ability to pray in tongues for personal edification.

The Benefits of Speaking with Tongues

There are several very powerful benefits given to the Christian when speaking or praying in tongues. Because of these benefits, you should develop a daily habit of praying in other tongues. Make it a part of your lifestyle to pray in the spirit.

Praying in the spirit:

1. **Builds up the inner man.**

   "He who speaks in a tongue edifies himself" (1 Corinthians 14:4). The inner man is the spirit and soul. When you pray in tongues, you edify or strengthen this inner man.

   One Greek scholar said that the word "edify" means to charge, as you would a battery. When we take the time to pray in the spirit, the inner man is charged up. You are ready to release power out of your innermost being (John 7:38-39).

2. **Allows us to receive revelation knowledge.**

"For anyone who speaks in a tongue does not speak to men but to God. Indeed, no one understands him; he utters mysteries with his spirit" (1 Corinthians 14:2).

The Father wants to share mysteries or divine secrets with us, but He cannot do it through our minds. We receive a real knowledge, not through a human spirit but through the Holy Spirit. When we pray in tongues on a regular basis, we open ourselves to the Holy Spirit to receive revelation knowledge of things that cannot be known by the natural mind alone.

Paul said, "I thank God that I speak in tongues more than all of you" (1 Corinthians 14:18). **Paul** definitely had more revelation knowledge than any other man.

3. **Enables you to hear the voice of your spirit.**

"For if I pray in a tongue, my spirit prays, but my mind is unfruitful" (1 Corinthians 14:14). Sometimes our greatest problem is our mind or the way we think. God does not lead men by their minds. He works through the human spirit (Proverbs 20:27). When we pray in tongues, our minds are not involved so we can hear our spirit.

4. Allows the spirit to pray for things you don't even know to pray for.

"In the same way, the Spirit helps us in our weakness. We do not know what we ought to pray, but the Spirit himself intercedes for us with groans that words cannot express" (Romans 8:26).

One of our greatest infirmities or weaknesses is not knowing how to pray. This is an inability to produce results, but the Holy Spirit wants to help us. When we are filled with the Spirit, He can pray through us with sounds that cannot be spoken in articulate speech—other tongues—and we will be praying for things that our natural minds don't even know about. This is one of the greatest tools of the believer: intercessory prayer in the Spirit.

5. **Allows us to pray the perfect will of God.**

"And he who searches our hearts knows the mind of the Spirit, because the Spirit intercedes for the saints in accordance with God's will" (Romans 8:27).

We all face situations when we don't know God's will, but the Holy Spirit always knows the will of God. When we pray for a specific thing in other tongues, we can be sure we are praying the perfect will of God. In tongues, there are no unbeliefs, no mistakes, and no failures.

6. **Builds up your faith.**

"But you, dear friends, build yourselves up on your most holy faith and pray in the Holy Spirit" (Jude 20).

This does not say tongues will give you faith, but praying in the Spirit will build you up on your faith. At times, you may sense that your faith is weak. If you will pray in the Spirit for a time, it will lift you up and then you can put your faith to work.

7. **Brings rest and refreshing.**

"Very well then, with foreign lips and strange tongues God will speak to this people, to whom he said, 'this is the resting place, let the weary rest;' and, 'this is the place of repose'—but they would not listen" (Isaiah 28:11-12).

Have you ever awoken after eight hours of sleep and still felt tired? It wasn't physical fatigue but fatigue in the inner man. Isaiah prophesied that praying in tongues will bring rest and refreshing to the inner man. Even after hours of work, if you spend time praying in tongues, you will begin to be refreshed.

8. **Helps us keep our tongue in line with the Word.**

"The tongue also is a fire, a world of evil among the parts of the body. It corrupts the whole person, sets the whole course of his life on fire, and is itself set on fire by hell. But no man can tame the tongue. It is a restless evil, full of deadly poison. With the tongue we praise our Lord and Father, and with it we curse men, who have been made in God's likeness. Out of the same mouth come praise and cursing. My brothers, they should not be" (James 3:6, 8-10).

You will have what you say, so it's important to say the right thing. Natural man cannot tame the tongue, but with the help of the Spirit of God, we can. When we pray in the Spirit, we are taming the tongue and submitting it to the Lord.

9. **Gives thanks and magnifies God.**

"Else when thou shalt bless with the spirit…for thou verily givest thanks well" (1 Corinthians 14:16-17, KJV).

"For they heard them speaking in tongues and praising God" (Acts 10:46).

There is no greater avenue of worship than the Spirit. Paul said he sang in the Spirit. Jesus said true worship was in the Spirit (John 4:24). If you have ever seen a body of Spirit-filled believers worshipping God, you can quickly see a tremendous difference.

10. Is a sign to unbelievers.

"Tongues, then, are sign, not for the believers but for the unbelievers; prophecy, however, is for believers, not for unbelievers" (1 Corinthians 14:22).

Many are worried about offending non-Christians in church so they don't allow speaking in tongues in the service. The Bible teaches that this sign will help the unbelievers to realize that God is present and His power is real. We shouldn't quench the gifts of God but encourage their manifestation.

How to Receive the Baptism with the Holy Spirit

Many people have prayed or had others pray for them to be filled with the Spirit but never receive anything. This situation often causes confusion, condemnation, or wrong thinking. Some have thought, *I must not be good enough,* or *God doesn't want me to have it.* God **does** want you to have it and here are some simple steps that will enable you to receive.

1. **Know that you are born again.**

   Only the born-again believer is a candidate for the baptism with the Holy Spirit. The world cannot receive this experience (Romans 10:9-10; John 14:17).

2. **Ask Jesus to baptize or fill you with the Spirit.**

He said in Luke 11:11-13, "Which of you fathers, if your son asks for a fish, will give him a snake instead? Or if he asks for an egg, will you give him a scorpion? If you then, though you are evil, know how to give good gifts to your children, how much more will your father in heaven give the Holy Spirit to those who ask him!"

3. **Believe that you received no matter how you feel or think.**

We receive from God **by faith, not feelings.** You don't have to feel anything to receive the Holy Ghost (Mark 11:24; Hebrews 11:6).

4. **Don't try to understand it with your mind.**

1 Corinthians 14:2 says, "For anyone who speaks in a tongue does not speak to men but to God. Indeed, no one understands him; he utters mysteries with his spirit."

Your mind will never understand tongues; it's not supposed to. This is a spiritual experience, not a mental one.

5. **After you've asked Jesus to fill you with the Holy Spirit, begin to speak sounds that are not your natural language.**

Your head will resist this and say, "It's foolish," "You're making this up," or use other reasoning, but this is not a mental experience. From your spirit, sounds will come that don't make sense. Open your mouth. Use your voice, lips, and tongue to speak them out. God does not speak with tongues, and He will not make you do it. Acts 2:4 says, "All of them were filled with the Holy Spirit and began to speak in other tongues as a spirit enabled them." **They** did the speaking, not the Holy Ghost.

6. **Relax and let yourself flow in the Spirit and pray boldly in other tongues for several minutes.**

Jesus said Satan will always try to steal what we receive from God (Mark 4:15). Don't let him steal from you. You may start thinking all kinds of funny thoughts or have doubts, but reject that thinking and believe the Bible. Remember, Jesus said if you ask, the Father will give you the Holy Ghost and, "These signs will accompany those who believe: In my name they will drive out demons; they will speak in new tongues" (Mark 16:17).

Praying in other tongues was a great blessing to the body of Christ. It is a gift that all believers should cultivate and use regularly. You'll find great spiritual enrichment and strength as you spend time daily praying in the Spirit. Remember these words of the Apostle Paul, "Therefore, my brothers, be eager to prophesy, and do not forbid speaking in tongues" (1 Corinthians 14:39).

THE NEXT STEP

This is just the beginning of your new life. These next few chapters will show you the specific areas to help you grow in your Christian walk.

Growing Up Spiritually

Being born again and baptized with the Holy Spirit is only the beginning. The Lord has many wonderful things for you as you grow in knowledge of the truth. Many times Christians don't realize they must grow and change. To be born again is just that: you are born. Now, just like a baby, you must grow up.

1 Peter 2:2 says, "Like newborn babies, crave pure spiritual milk, so that by it you may grow up in your salvation." The King James Version translation says, "Desire the sincere milk of the Word that ye may grow thereby."

By growing in knowledge of the Word of God, you will receive the spiritual food you need to grow up into spiritual maturity. Many people are born again but never eat spiritual food so they do not grow. Imagine what would happen to a small baby if it had no mother to feed it. It would be only a few days until the child starved to death. So it is with the spiritual babe. You must be fed a steady diet of the Word of God in order to grow in the Lord. Jesus said in John 8:23, "If you hold on to my teaching (Word), you are really my disciples. Then you will know the truth, and the truth will set you free."

If there are areas in your life that make you feel as if you are in bondage, the truth will set you free. Many things cannot be prayed away or pushed aside, but by learning the truth you can change things and be free. Jesus desires for you to be happy, healthy, and free. If there are problems in your life, the truth will enable you to overcome them and live the abundant life (John 10:10).

We read in 2 Timothy 3:16-17, "All Scripture is God-breathed and is useful for teaching, rebuking, correcting and training the righteous, so that the man of God may be thoroughly equipped for every good work."

The Scriptures of the Word of God have been inspired by the Father. That means He spoke through men to give us the Bible. His Word is profitable to us for teaching, correcting, and training for our successful Christian life. The reason many people suffer through life with problems and miseries is that they don't understand the principles of the Bible. Notice that this verse tells us that the Word will prepare or equip us for **every good work.** By growing in knowledge of the Scriptures, we will be preparing for every aspect of Christian living.

Another vitally important part of growing up spiritually is going to church. You must find a church that will teach the Bible simply, clearly, and with authority. Jesus always spoke simply so people could understand. If someone is speaking "over your head," it will not help you grow.

Paul said in Hebrews 10:25, "Let us not give up meeting together, as some are in the habit of doing, but let us encourage one another—and all the more as you see the Day approaching."

Become involved with a fired-up church that you feel you can grow in. They should be helping people to be filled with the Holy Spirit and speaking with new tongues, laying hands on the sick, and ministering to the needs of people. Through regular Bible teaching, you will be spiritually strengthened. It will not happen overnight, but if you are consistent, growth will come.

Bible Reading Plan

The Bible has so much information that many times we become lost trying to figure out where to begin, so I'll give you a simple plan to start learning the Word.

First, read through the book of Galatians in two different translations (i.e., New International Version and King James Version). Don't read so fast that it does not make any sense. There is no value in just reading a lot of Scripture. The important thing is to gain knowledge and understanding.

Second, read through the book of James in two different translations. This will cause you to gain insight concerning faith and Christian behavior.

As you read and think about these two books, the Lord will help you understand how to deal with the things you face daily. If you have questions or points of confusion, do not hesitate to talk to other

Christians or your pastor. After you have read those books two times each, go back to the first book of the New Testament, Matthew, and read each book in order. Remember, do not try to get through as fast as possible.

Take time to meditate, ponder, or think on Scriptures so you can understand them. Just saying "I read the whole New Testament" will not impress God. It is growing in knowledge and understanding that will help you.

Renewing Your Mind

Many people do not realize that the Christian Life is one of change. That means you must be willing to give up your way of thinking and accept God's way of thinking. Every time you think in a way that is contrary to the Word, make a decision to give up your thoughts and accept God's thoughts. Romans 12:2 says, “Do not conform any longer to the pattern of this world, but be transformed by the renewing of your mind. Then you will be able to test and approve what God's will is—his good, pleasing and perfect will.”

Notice that your mind must be renewed to do the will of God. You will find many areas in your life, such as relationships, money, health, faith, talking, and responsibility, that you will have to change. As you learn the Word of God, these areas will become apparent to you and you can change your thinking.

Don't try to make excuses or prove yourself right. Be willing to change. In this way, God will be able to bless your life and there will be a steady increase of spiritual growth. Here again, it will not happen all at once. This is a never-ending process.

The mind that is not renewed to the Word of God will stop you from walking with the Lord. In Romans 12:2, Paul said to be approved or do the will of God, you must be transformed. The English word "transform" comes from the Greek word "metamorphoo." It means to change into another form. Every born-again person has thinking that must be changed. As this happens, the mind is renewed and the good, pleasing, and perfect will of God will then be fulfilled.

Paul said again in 2 Corinthians 10:4-5, "The weapons we fight with are not the weapons of the world. On the contrary, they have divine power to demolish strongholds. We demolish arguments and every pretension that sets itself up against the knowledge of God, and we take captive every thought to make it obedient to Christ."

From the Scripture, we see that our enemy Satan attempts to build up strongholds in our lives. These strongholds are thoughts and ideas that are contrary to the truth and keep us from a happy Christian life. Paul tells us to pull down every imagination (reasoning) and get "every thought" in line with Jesus or the Word of God. It is possible to control your thoughts and keep your thinking on positive things.

The enemy will try to put thoughts of doubt, confusion, or negativity in your mind, but as you continue to replace your old way of thinking with the truth, the joy and peace of the Lord will grow strong in you. Romans 8:5-8, says, "Those who live according to the sinful nature have their mind set on what the nature desires; but those who live in accordance with the Spirit have their mind set on what the Spirit desires. The mind of sinful man is death, but the mind controlled by the Spirit is life in peace, because the sinful mind is hostile to God. It does not submit to God's law, nor can it do so. Those controlled by the sinful nature cannot please God."

The mind can either agree with the flesh or sinful nature and you will do what it desires, or the mind can agree with your spirit and you will do what the Holy Spirit desires. Your life has three parts to it: the flesh, the soul (mind, emotions, and will), and the spirit. The flesh contacts the natural world and is where the sinful desires of man exist. The spirit contacts God and becomes a new creation when you are born again. The mind can go whichever way you decide or "will" for it to go. The mind can follow the flesh and negativity, which leads to death, or you can renew your mind and make it follow the Spirit, which is life in peace. You have the ability to control your thoughts and keep them on positive things. At first, it may seem hard, but as you grow, it will be easier and the benefits will be greater.

Bible Confessions

A part of renewing your mind to the Spirit of God is choosing what you say. The Bible states that what you say can preserve life or destroy it (Proverbs 18:21), so you must be aware of the consequences of your words. Remember that you choose whether your mind will line up with your flesh nature or with the Spirit of God. Confessing the Word of God aloud helps to direct that choice.

Bible confessions are simply listing together several Bible verses in a way that you can confess the truth of God's Word over your life. Here are some scriptural confessions for you to say over your life. Read one or two of these aloud every single day and start creating a new pattern of speaking as you continue to grow spiritually.

Personal Commitment and Discipline

I am a disciplined man/woman of God. I give myself continually to prayer and to the ministry of God, a workman who need not be ashamed, rightly dividing the Word of truth. I am not conformed to this world but transformed by the renewing of my mind to prove what is that good, acceptable, and perfect will of God. I am risen with Christ. I set my mind on things above, not on the things on this earth. I seek those things which are above where Christ sits on the right hand of God. Whatsoever things are true, honest, just, pure, lovely, of good report, virtuous, and praiseworthy, these are the only things on which I fix my mind.

I love (*spouse's name)* as Jesus loved the church, and gave Himself for it. We walk in harmony and in one accord. We have been made one by the Spirit of God. I love (*children's names)*. I train them in the way they should go, and when they are old they will not depart from it. I raise them up in the nurture and the admonition of the Lord.

My body is the temple of the Holy Spirit. There shall no evil befall me, neither shall any plague come near my dwelling. By the stripes of Jesus I am healed. I am blessed with the blessings of Abraham. I am very rich in silver and in gold. The blessing of the Lord makes me rich and He adds no sorrow to it. I prosper and live in health even as my soul prospers. As He who has called me is holy, so I am holy in all manner of lifestyle because it is written, "Be holy for I am holy."

I put off concerning the former conduct, the old man, which is corrupt according to the deceitful lusts. I am renewed in the spirit of my mind and put on the new man which after God is created in righteousness and true holiness. I am strong and very courageous. The Word of God shall not depart out of my mouth, but I meditate therein day and night to observe to do according to all that is written therein. Then I make my way prosperous and then I have good success.

Genesis 49:26 (AMP); Joshua 1:7-8; Psalm 91:10; Proverbs 10:22; Proverbs 22:6; Acts 6:4; Romans 12:2; 1 Corinthians 3:16; Ephesians 4:22-24; Ephesians 5:25; Ephesians 6:4; Philippians 4:8; Colossians 3:1-2; 2 Timothy 2:15; 1 Peter 1:15-16; 1 Peter 2:24

Wisdom, Knowledge, and the Direction of God

I do not seek after riches, wealth, or honor, but I seek for wisdom and knowledge that are granted unto me, and I believe You have given riches, wealth, and honor according to Your Word. Wisdom is the principal thing, therefore I get wisdom, and with all my getting I get understanding. I exalt Wisdom and she promotes me. She'll bring me to honor when I embrace her.

Happy is the man who finds wisdom and the man who gets understanding, for the merchandise of it is better than the merchandise of silver, and the gain thereof than fine gold. Wisdom is more precious than rubies and all the things I can desire are not to be compared to her. Length of days is in her right hand and in her left hand is riches and honor. She is the tree of life to them that lay hold upon her. Happy is everyone who retains her. The Lord by wisdom has founded the earth, by understanding has He established the heavens. I am willing and obedient, and I eat the best the land has to offer. I seek first the kingdom of God and His righteousness, and all these other things are added unto me. I am a blessed man/woman who walks not in the counsel of the ungodly, nor stands in the way of sinners, nor sits in the seat of the scornful. But my delight is in the law of the Lord, and in Your law do I meditate day and night. I am like a tree planted by rivers of water that brings forth fruit in season. My leaf also shall not wither and whatever I do shall prosper.

2 Chronicles 1:12; Psalm 1:1-3; Proverbs 3:13-19; Proverbs 4:7-8; Isaiah 1:19; Matthew 6:33

Ministry

The Spirit of the Lord is upon me because He has anointed me to preach the gospel to the poor. He has sent me to heal the brokenhearted, to preach deliverance to the captives, and the recovering of sight to the blind, to set at liberty those who are bruised, and to preach the acceptable year of the Lord. Jesus is made unto me wisdom, righteousness, sanctification, and redemption. If I lack wisdom, I ask of God who gives to all men liberally and without reproach, and it is given to me. I walk in love. The love of God is shed abroad in my heart by the Holy Spirit. I have been made in the righteousness of God in Christ. Whatever I do shall prosper, for I prosper and live in health, even as my soul prospers. I tread on serpents and scorpions and over all the power of the enemy. Nothing shall by any means hurt me, for the joy of the Lord is my strength.

Luke 4:18; Luke 10:19; Romans 5:5; 1 Corinthians 1:30; 2 Corinthians 5:21; James 1:5; 3 John 2; Nehemiah 8:10

Now that you are born again, continue to grow up in the Lord by being baptized with water, filled with the Holy Spirit, and continually renewing your mind. This new life has many wonderful things in store for you.

BE YOU THROUGH JESUS
A 7-DAY DEVOTIONAL

Day 1: A Brand New Life

John 3:3:

"Jesus answered and said to him, 'Most assuredly, I say to you, unless one is born again, he cannot see the kingdom of God.'"

This is a big day and an important step in your story. Yes, you have a great story. Your life is unique, important, and amazing. What God has brought you through to this point is something no one else has done in quite the same way; you are UNIQUE. Your life is IMPORTANT to God and to the many people you will touch throughout your years with Him. It is and will be AMAZING how you will influence others and be a blessing as you walk with God.

Think of the three parts of your story:

1. What you have come through to get here today;

2. How having Jesus, in your life, can heal and change the things you do in your future; and

3. What your destiny can be with Him.

It may be just a thought in your heart, but let the Lord enlarge that thought of what the future has for you and those around you. Begin to see yourself growing in God and growing stronger in a daily relationship with Jesus.

Scripture Readings:

John 5:24

Ephesians 2:10

Ephesians 6:10

Romans 3:23

Romans 6:23

Romans 10:9

Ask Yourself:

1. How do I see myself growing in God and growing in His Word?

2. What are some challenges from my past that I'd like to move forward from?

3. What area of life do I desire to have God help me grow stronger in?

Day 2: You Have Family

1 Corinthians 12:27, (The Message):
"You are Christ's body—that's who you are! You must never forget this. Only as you accept your part of that body does your 'part' mean anything."

You are not alone. If you have felt alone before or feel that way in the coming days, remember you are a part of God's family—an important and integral part of God's family. This family is worldwide AND it's right here at Christian Faith (CF) for you. The Bible calls this family the "Body of Christ."

We are all members of one body who work together and make each part important. Separate, we may not accomplish much on this earth; but together in unity and harmony, we can do great things.

As a part of His church and His body, you are an important member and will have many things that you can both give and receive. Don't stay alone. Get involved. Make friends. Find a place where you can serve.

The devil would love for you to stay isolated and disconnected from the whole, but God has called us all to unity. Take a risk and be bold and see how enriching it can be in your life.

Scripture Readings:

Psalm 68:6

Romans 12:4-5

1 Corinthians 12:12

John 14:26

Acts 1:8

Acts 2:4

1 Corinthians 14:2, 14-15

Luke 11:13

Jude 20

Ask Yourself:

1. What can I do to get more involved in my church family?

2. What are some of the fears that would try to keep me from getting involved, and how can I overcome them?

3. What abilities, skills, and strengths do I have that I might use to help others?

Day 3: Share Your Story

2 Corinthians 5:19-20 (The Message):

"God has given us the task of telling everyone what He is doing. We're Christ's representatives. God uses us to persuade men and women to drop their differences and enter into God's work of making things right between them. We're speaking for Christ himself now: Become friends with God; he's already a friend with you."

You have a voice. You have something that your friends and family need to hear. You may feel as if you aren't the one who should say anything, but you are the best person, and maybe the only one, to tell those in your life about Jesus. Could you tell them what you felt and what you experienced at church? Or maybe it's time to tell them about what you believe and what you have realized is in the Bible.

Sharing the message of Jesus doesn't have to be spiritually complicated. Simply share your words and your perspective on what the Bible and Church are to you. The sooner you tell them, the better.

You may not know yet how your heart has been changed and how the Spirit in you will impact those around you. Don't hold Him back; let the love out!

Jesus taught His disciples that as they opened their mouth to share His message, the Holy Spirit would give them ideas and words that would help the people they were talking to. The Lord will use you in the very same way. Your voice and your words are important.

Scripture Readings:

Mark 5:19

1 Corinthians 9:16

1 Peter 4:11

1 Corinthians 12:18

Hebrews 10:24-25

Psalm 92:13

Ask Yourself:

1. Who are the people in my life who need Jesus, and how can I share Jesus with them today?

2. What could I say to my friends and family to help them know Jesus?

3. In which areas can I ask God for more confidence to help me effectively represent Him?

Day 4: We Are Better Together

Proverbs 18:1:

"A man who isolates himself seeks his own desire; He rages against all wise judgment."

There is a place for you in God's church. Any church can seem big and you may feel as if everyone knows each other, but that isn't true. It is certainly not the case at Christian Faith. We want you and need you in our church family. There are small groups for relationships, growth, and discipleship; and large groups for worship, celebration, and experiencing the Lord as one. You are important to the life of our church, and we need you. As you stay connected and keep taking steps to be involved, you will see there is a place for you and that your input is immeasurable.

CF is structured through two main groups: large gatherings and small groups. The large gatherings are the main weekend services. The small groups are held around our communities in small get-togethers. Both are valuable and enrich our lives to make us stronger in the Lord.

The Bible teaches that we all help each other to become more like Jesus. Alone and isolated, we don't grow. But together as the Body of Christ, the Church, we all do better.

Scripture Readings:

Proverbs 27:17

Acts 2:46-47

Romans 8:29

Romans 12:1-2

Ephesians 4:22-24

Colossians 3:1-2

Ask Yourself:

1. Am I nervous to get involved in church because of the size?

2. If so, what can I do to take a step toward getting connected, either through the large gatherings or small groups?

Day 5: You Are Designed by God... Be You

2 Corinthians 5:17-18:

"Therefore if any man be in Christ, he is a new creature: old things are passed away; behold, all things are become new. And all things are of God, who hath reconciled us to himself by Jesus Christ, and hath given to us the ministry of reconciliation."

You can BE YOU! You are not here to become like someone else, other than Jesus. We want you to BE YOU. You are part of God's plan for someone's future. There are people you know or people you will know that you can influence for God as you speak into their lives. No one else can say what you can say in the way you say it. Your story is unique, and God will use it in unique ways.

Don't think you need to be like other people. Be yourself and believe that you have a wonderful destiny. As you grow in the Lord and become the person He designed, you'll see God's plan for your life unfolding and you'll walk in His blessing.

It's human nature to be dissatisfied with ourselves. We are told that we aren't good enough, smart enough, or strong enough, but those are lies. When we believe the lies of the devil, we feel inferior.

At CF, our message is simple: BE YOU. God created you! As we embrace this truth with perfect confidence, we'll live bigger and better lives for Jesus.

Scripture Readings:

Psalm 139:14

Proverbs 4:11

Mark 13:11

Psalm 119:11

John 8:31-32

Romans 10:17

Ask Yourself:

1. What does BE YOU mean to me, and how have I been dissatisfied with myself?

2. In what ways have I tried to be someone else?

3. What are some ways that God has made me unique?

Day 6: There Is No Easy Road

James 1:2-4:

"My brethren, count it all joy when you fall into various trials, knowing that the testing of your faith produces patience. But let patience have its perfect work, that you may be perfect and complete, lacking nothing."

Being a Christian is not always easy. There will be challenges because you have an enemy—the devil. Of course, doing anything worthwhile is not easy. As a husband, wife, father, or mother, you are challenged to grow and change. So it is as a Christian. You will be challenged in your faith and what you believe in various ways.

Sometimes you won't know what to believe or how to feel about things. Don't worry; trust that God will lead and guide you through every challenge. As you stay relaxed and know He loves you, you will grow through the challenges of life.

It never seems like it's happening fast enough, but you are getting stronger. Day by day you are growing in Him.

Through every storm and challenge, have perfect confidence that God will never leave you. He promises two things: storms will come, and He won't leave you. If the storm is longer than you think it should be, remind yourself that God is with you and keep pressing forward.

Scripture Readings:

Matthew 7:13-14

Romans 8:18

2 Corinthians 4:17

Psalm 103:2-3

John 8:10-11

1 John 1:9

Ask Yourself:

1. Have there been storms in life that caused me to question if God was still with me?

2. How can I be confident now knowing that God will never leave me?

Day 7: God Has a Plan for You

Psalm 23:1-3:

"The Lord is my shepherd; I shall not want. He makes me to lie down in green pastures; He leads me beside the still waters. He restores my soul…"

The Lord is good. He has a good plan for your life. As you learn the Bible and grow in Him, His plan will become clearer in your life and it will be good. Don't give up or be distracted by the attractions we see through the media, news, sports, and this world. The god of this world, Satan, would like to keep you from walking with God. Sometimes his greatest tactics are to simply keep us busy and distracted.

Don't let yourself be so distracted by the world that you lose focus on the good plans God has for you. You are on your journey with Him. Stay patient and know that God has small and big blessings in store for you. He will never leave you, and He promises that He has not forgotten the desires of your heart. God is working things out even before we see them coming to pass.

Keep praying, learning His Word, and growing in His church, and you will be on your way to abundant life: abundant blessings in your spirit, soul, and body.

Scripture Readings:

Jeremiah 29:11

1 Corinthians 15:58

Philippians 1:6

Ask Yourself:

1. How have I seen God at work in my life already?

2. In what ways have I allowed the attractions of a worldly lifestyle to distract me from pursuing the life God has for me?

A catalog of additional materials by Casey and Wendy Treat can be found at www.CaseyTreat.com.

Made in the USA
Columbia, SC
22 January 2025

52157881R00057